Steve Williams

Leadership

Maximize Your Potential and Lead Like You Were Born To!

Steve Williams

D1282525

i

Steve Williams

Contents

Introduction

I want to thank you and congratulate you for buying the book, *Leadership – Maximize Your Potential and Lead like You Were Born To!*

This book contains everything you need to know to be an effective, efficient leader who will inspire people to follow you. Many people think that they are either born to be a leader or that they aren't, but truthfully, anyone can learn to be a leader. Being an effective leader is more than just a thought process. You need to understand how to communicate well, and you also need to be able to organize groups of people in a way that works for everyone.

Chapter 1 - What is Leadership?

Many times, we see people in a leadership position and it seems like they really have no idea what leadership is or how to be a truly successful leader. In this chapter, I want to quickly go over what leadership is and what a successful leader looks like.

Most people believe leadership is nothing more than the act of leading a group of people in some activity, but that could not be further from the truth. There are also those who lead from the sidelines, meaning they do not take part in the activity, but instead, tend to tell everyone else what to do.

The truth is, when you are a true leader, you will be involved in the activity, each person you are leading will be in the best position according to their skills and talents and you will not have to tell people what to do or micromanage because they will be following your lead.

After all, that is what it is all about. When you are a leader, your job is to get people to follow your lead, not do what you say simply because you said for them to do it. Asking what leadership is may seem like a very simple question, but in fact, it is a very complex question that deserves a deeper look.

Leadership is going to mean a lot of different things to a lot of different people. In fact, if you ask 100 people what leadership means to them, chances are, you are going to get 100 different answers. So, to define leadership, you need to ask yourself what leadership means to you.

Some people define leadership as the ability to move a group of people toward a specific goal, others define it as directing people through a specific activity, and still others feel that leadership is being able to direct the actions of people by serving their needs.

Personally, I feel that leadership is actually all three. When you are a true leader, you are able to move a group of people through direction through the activity that you want them to accomplish while focusing on the needs of the people. What would this look like in a real-life situation?

Let's take a look at two scenarios: The first one is going to be about a manager at a local store. She always seems to be in a bad mood, she slams products around, is rude to customers, and talks about them behind their backs. This same manager expects all of her employees to show up for work each day with a smile on their face, she does not want any complaints from customers about her employees, and she wants them to get all of their work done without having an attitude.

This specific store has seen a lot of turnover in employees. Most of the cashiers are in a bad mood the majority of the time, they show no respect to the manager, and it is reflected in the condition of the store. The manager does not understand what is going on and tends to blame the employees for the issues instead of looking at her own leadership skills.

Now let's think about this same store and imagine the manager decided to lead her employees by working hard in the store and by displaying a positive attitude. We will imagine that she was polite to customers and treated them and the employees with respect. She also ensured that those employees who had the best people skills were behind the counter while those who were not so people-friendly were busy stocking the shelves. Instead of blaming everyone else for the conditions of the store, she took responsibility for her leadership skills and focused on making changes.

Can you imagine the difference that would be seen in the store? Chances are, the store would start getting more business, employees would stay longer and be much happier, and the manager would not feel as if everything was falling down on her shoulders.

The fact is that if you are in a leadership position and you feel like you are having to do everything, or that you are having to fight with those who you are leading to get them to do the things you need them to do, then you are doing it wrong.

You see, people naturally want to please other people. They want the approval of those who are in higher positions and they want to feel as if they are appreciated. When people feel as if they are not respected and they do not matter to the people who are higher up than they are, they are not going to follow those people.

Think about it this way: The manager who worked at the store in scenario one struggles with her job every day and is in a terrible mood. Would you want to follow someone who displayed the types of behavior she does? Of course not, no one wants to be miserable all of the time and if the leader cannot take control over their own jobs, how are those who are supposed to follow her trust that they are leading them correctly?

A true leader is able to convince people to invest their time, money, and skills toward a specific goal. In a way, they are a salesperson for their cause, even if the cause is simply getting employees to do their job or not quit the job they currently have.

Real leaders come from all walks of life and they lead in many different ways, but the common attribute of all true leaders is that they believe a specific action needs to be taken and they take the steps to get those they are leading to complete that specific action.

A true leader does not need to use threats to get people to follow them, they do not need to punish people or humiliate them. Instead, a true leader leads by example. If a true leader wants those they are leading to have a certain standard then they set that standard and stick to it. They do not allow themselves to fall below that standard and by doing so, they are showing those who are following them that not only is it possible to reach that standard, but it is possible to maintain it as well.

If you have ever worked in a factory, then you will understand that when the boss is out on the floor and working just as hard as the employees, quality is high, as is production, but when you have a boss who sits in the office with their feet propped up on their desks and watches everyone else work, quality is low as is production.

No matter what area you are leading people in, the same principle will apply. If you are involved, you are going to get better results than if you sit back and dictate how things should be done.

Of course, there is much more to being a great leader than simply getting involved and we will discuss this further in later chapters. I simply want you to start focusing on what a great leader looks like.

Sit back in your seat and close your eyes. Think about what it would look like if you were a great leader. How would you behave? What would you accomplish? What would it look like to actually lead instead of dictating?

As we move into the next chapter and throughout the rest of this book, I want you to keep that idea in your mind. As we learn more, your visualization will change and you will begin to see how you can actually become that great leader you want to be.

Chapter 2 - Leadership Qualities

Learning how to be a great leader is not something you can simply read about and do. To be a great leader, you are going to have to make some changes within yourself. The first step is understanding that the changes need to be made with you, not with those you are leading. By making the changes within yourself, you will find that those you are leading will make the changes needed as well.

Of course, there are always going to be those few who refuse to make any changes and even fight against any type of change. These are the people who need to be removed from your team as quickly as possible.

The question remains, what are the qualities of a true leader? If you want to get people to follow you and not just do what you tell them to, then you have to possess a few qualities. Of course, you do not have to have all of the qualities that I will talk about and you do not have to be perfect, but one quality of a true leader is that they are always looking for the chance to learn more and improve themselves.

The next quality I want to talk about is being honest. If you want to be a great leader, then those who follow you must believe they can trust you. If your followers do not feel they can trust you, they will quit following you pretty quickly. I remember this happening to one man I worked with. At first, everyone thought that he was a great leader, he helped to implement a lot of change in the workplace and things were going great. That was until he got a taste of what it felt like to be in charge and have people look up to you. It was at that point that he began sharing conversations that were had with him in private and employees were getting reprimanded for the things they had talked about. That was when he lost the trust of his followers. People stopped helping him and his entire program fell apart. Trust is one of the most important qualities a leader can have.

This leads me into the next quality and that is that a leader will not abuse the authority that is given to him. People catch on pretty quickly and when they notice you abusing your authority, they no longer look at you as a leader but as a dictator. This is when things tend to fall apart and the once leader has to do all of the work on their own. It is important for a true leader to stay humble and understand that the success or failure of any project is up to them. If the project fails, it is not the fault of the followers, but instead, it is the fault of the leader.

A true leader builds others up. One thing many micromanagers do is break other people down.

They point out their faults and never give a compliment, all the while, expecting those who they are supposed to be leading to work even harder for them. The problem with this is that when you break people down, they do not want to do anything for you. On the other hand, when you build people up and compliment the work they have done, they only want to work harder to receive more compliments. People respond to praise and a true leader understands that. As leaders, we need to remember that people do the things they do because they are benefiting from it in some way. When a person receives a compliment or is shown appreciation, they will continue to work hard because they want to feel good about themselves. On the other hand, when they are constantly talked down to, or told that their work is not good enough, they are going to give up because they are not benefiting from the actions they are doing. Even if the person is being paid for their work, it is not enough. Their leader has to show them that they are appreciated.

A successful leader is optimistic. You will never find a successful leader who is always looking at the bad side of everything, who is always in a bad mood and who screams and yells. Quite the opposite. The leaders you meet who are successful in what they do are going to be positive people, they are going to be people who want to share their knowledge with others and who understand that people fail. They are going to be the people who look for teachable moments when those who are following them do fail and they are going to be those leaders who lift their followers up to their level.

A true leader is someone who teaches by example. We discussed this a bit in the previous chapter, but it is very important and it is one of the qualities that all successful leaders must have. A successful leader does not sit in their office with their feet propped on a desk and dictate to their followers what needs to be done but instead, they are the example for their followers. A real leader will get up out of their chair, out of their office, and show those they are in charge of leading exactly how things are done.

A successful leader knows their own limitations as well as those of the people they are in charge of leading. One of the reasons many people fail is because they set their expectations far too high, not only for themselves, but also for those who they are supposed to be leading. This is not to say that you should set low expectations, but instead, it means you need to understand what your limitations are. You should also understand that those you are in charge of have limitations as well. You cannot expect people to focus on any specific project for hours upon hours, seven days a week. You have to remember that just like you, those you are in charge of get tired, they need breaks and they need excitement.

Any leader who is successful has a lot of self-discipline. It is very easy to get caught up in conversation when a meeting is supposed to be going on and lose track of half of your day. It is also easy to not focus on the task at hand and forget about the progress that needs to be made, but a true leader does not allow this to happen. A successful leader knows how to keep the attention of those they are in charge of leading and they know that if the work is not done, it is their own fault. A self-disciplined leader is one who reminds themselves, and those they are in charge of, that the specific activity needs to be completed and does not allow anything to get in their way. Self-discipline is something that comes with a lot of practice so do not feel bad if you find that you fail quite often when you are trying to practice it. It can take years to build up the self-discipline you need to become a great leader, but that does not mean you cannot lead while you are learning.

The last characteristic of a true leader I want to talk about is that a successful leader uses good judgement. The leader learns how to read people and is able to tell which people will work well together. They are able to find the skills and talents within people and use them to help ensure the project's success. They are able to judge their progress as well as the progress of those they are leading without any bias.

Being a leader is not something that you can simply decide you want to do one day and then be successful at it. It takes a lot of work as well as a lot of learning for you to be a successful leader. You have to know how to relate to people, how to understand people, how to motivate people, and how to keep people's attention. More than anything, you need to know how to take control of yourself, your own life, your own job, your own emotions, and every other area of your life that those you are leading may be looking at.

The reason for this is because no one is going to respect a leader who is trying to lead a group of people and does not have a good handle on their own life. Here is an example:

Each week, a group of people meet. They all want to lose weight and get in shape, but when they meet for the first time, they find that their leader is overweight, smokes, drinks heavily, and has not eaten a vegetable in the past 10 years. Yes, the person is their leader and they can have all of the other characteristics that a good leader should have, but do you think that anyone is going to take what that person has to say to heart? No, they are going to look at that person and ask why he or she should be leading them when they can't even take care of themselves.

It may seem blunt and it may seem a bit mean, but I am not here to sugar coat anything. This book is to help you become a successful leader, not to help you feel better about the leader you are.

This same issue can show up in any area of our lives. It does not matter if you are a leader in a church, at work, at school, or even in your own home, if you do not have yourself in order, no one is going to listen to what you have to say or do what you would like them to do.

Chapter 3 - Strategies and Techniques of a Successful Leader

Knowing the characteristics of a successful leader is simply not enough to make you the successful leader you want to be. To be a truly successful leader, there are some steps you need to take and in this chapter, I want to discuss not only the steps that you need to take to be a successful leader but also the strategies and techniques successful leaders use.

If you want to be a successful leader, you need to have a mission statement. You should actually have several mission statements for different areas in your life as well as the different areas you are serving as a leader in. For example, if you are a parent, you are leading your children and you should have a mission statement. If you are a leader in your church, you should have a mission statement. If you are a leader at work you also need a mission statement, or maybe you are a leader in an industry, or you are known as a guru. In any of these cases, you need to have a mission statement that is specific for each area.

There is no set guidelines for writing a mission statement, but here are a few tips to help you:

1. Ensure that the statement is simple and clear. It should be no more than five sentences long.

2. The mission statement should state what you want to focus on and how it will affect a specific area of your life.

3. The statement should be positive. Don't state what you don't want to do, but instead, focus on what the outcome will be.

4. Include the behaviors that you will need to focus on to reach your goal.

5. Ensure that the statement will help to guide your daily life. Incorporate the statement in your day-to-day life.

6. Ensure that the mission statement does not conflict with any of your personal beliefs or any other area of your life.

7. Put your emotions into the statement. Make sure the statement is full of passion.

8. Remember that your mission statement is not written in stone and can be changed at any time to align with your goals and your life. It does not have to be perfect, but it should direct you toward your goal each day.

The next step you need to take is to surround yourself with the right people. If you surround yourself with those who are great leaders, you will naturally become a great leader. On the other hand, if you surround yourself with those who have no leadership ability, then neither will you. You want to surround yourself with different types of people who have different points of view. You don't have to agree with everything they think, but you need to open yourself up to learning what they have to teach. The people you surround yourself with should be able to share their wisdom and insights with you.

Learning is something I will continue to mention throughout this book and that I have already mentioned once. If you want to be a great leader, you need to empower yourself with all of the knowledge you can get. If you are the type of person who loves continually learning, then this will not be a problem for you, but if you do not enjoy learning new things, it could cause some issues. You should create a goal to read one new book each week and I am not talking about some fantasy fiction book. What I am talking about is a book that helps you to improve who you are, one that teaches you about others, or one that simply teaches you a new skill. One trait that many great leaders share is that they have an extensive vocabulary. Try learning a new word every day or even every week. Always be expanding your mind.

If you want to be a successful leader, then you have to be willing to work hard. Success does not come easy. If it did, everyone would be successful and no one would ever worry about improving one's self. But we all know that to be successful, we have to work very hard. This does not mean you have to take on all of the responsibilities on your own and you should never be afraid to ask anyone for help; after all, the worst that could happen is that they say no. What I mean by this is that being a leader is not easy. It takes a lot of work and being a successful leader takes even more work, although, in the long run, those you are leading will be more likely to work on their own without you having to micromanage them. Most of the work you will be doing will be on yourself.

Truly great leaders take the time to invest in others. Not only do they invest their time in others, but they often times invest their money in them as well. You don't have to give people a bunch of money to invest in them, but when you are able, you should take the time to teach others how to be a great leader just as you are.

Another thing a true leader will do is to serve others. Remember when I told you that many people look at being a great leader as the ability to serve those who they are leading? This does not only mean that you should serve those you are leading but you should serve those who are less fortunate as well. When we serve, we are humbled and as I already stated it is very important for a successful leader to remain humble.

To be a successful leader, you also have to be quick to respond. This means that when those you are leading have a question, you quickly supply them with an answer. When you receive phone calls or emails, you need to respond to them quickly and ensure that you do not put them off. This is part of self-discipline but it also ensures that those you are leading, as well as those you are working with, feel valued.

One of the most important things you can do when you are a leader is to treat everyone the way that you want to be treated yourself. This is something we are taught at a very young age, but many of us tend to forget as we get older or as we move into positions of power. We forget that we were once the people who were being led and we tend to follow in our leader's footsteps. If you did not have a truly successful leader and you follow in their footsteps, chances are, you will not treat everyone the same way you want to be treated.

Remember to avoid greed at all costs. This is another pitfall of being successful, but if you are a successful leader, you will avoid the greed. Greed is not only about the money that you earn from any project you are in charge of but it also involves the recognition. Remind yourself how you would feel if you worked day after day to ensure the success of a project and the leader took all of the credit. Remember to always put yourself in the other person's position and consider how you would feel if the same thing happened to you. You should also understand that when people are recognized for helping you reach your goals, they will be more apt to help you when you need them again.

A true leader teaches those who they are in charge of to go above and beyond the expectations. It does not matter what type of project you are leading, or who you are leading the project for. If you go above and beyond, not only will you be teaching those you are leading what a good work ethic is but you will also be ensuring that you are able to lead future projects.

Of course, these are just a few steps that you need to take if you are going to be a great leader and once you have implemented these steps, you will want to move forward and take more advanced steps.

Next, I want to talk about five strategies that you can use to ensure that you are a successful leader. The first strategy is to make sure that your culture is a priority. Now, I am not talking about the culture that you are from but the culture of the group you are leading. For example, many factories have now chosen to create a winning culture and nurture the team environment. Many of these cultures expect people to act as owners in the area they are responsible for. This allows everyone to feel that they are important and it ensures that they are providing the best work possible. Whatever culture you decide you want, you need to make sure that you are spending time on developing that culture within your group.

Ensuring that the group has a positive vision is another strategy that many great leaders use. It does not matter what your goal is, there is always a way to put a positive spin on things. Instead of focusing on the negative, you simply need to reword your vision so it reflects the positive outcome you are looking for. One thing you will learn about great leaders is that they are not negative people. The majority of the most successful leaders in the world spend time focusing on the positive even when negative things are happening to them or their group. For this reason, you need to make sure that you can turn a negative situation into a positive outcome. One example of this could be that you are in charge of a safety group. You are supposed to lead the group to come up with ways to keep employees safe because there have been a lot of accidents lately. Instead of focusing on the accidents and bringing all of the negativity into your group, you need to focus on what the outcome will be, ensuring the safety of their fellow employees.

It is very easy to get caught up in the negative in any situation, but if you spend some time focusing on the positive, it will become more and more natural. I suggest that all great leaders take part in positive meditation, affirmations, and remove as much negativity from their lives as possible. You need to remember that our lives do not stop simply because we are in charge of leading others. If there is negativity anywhere in your personal life, it is going to come to light when you are leading a group of people. The reason for this is that leading is very stressful and when we become stressed, our true selves show. No matter how much you try to hide your negativity, it will eventually come out when you are leading a group of people. This is why it is best that you simply remove the negativity from your life.

This is not always an easy task and it does require some work, but it is possible to take a mostly negative person and turn them into a mostly positive person. The way that this is done is to begin by removing the negative influences in your life, then you will begin focusing on the positive things instead of all of the negative. The more positive things you focus on, the more positive things you will notice. Eventually, and I am talking about months down the road, you will not have to force yourself to focus on the positive, but will see a change within yourself and you will begin focusing on the positive things naturally.

This is what you want to bring to the group you are leading.

If the leader of a group is a positive person, then the group is going to be mostly positive and you will have a positive outcome. On the other hand, if the leader is negative, you will have a group that is full of negativity, murmuring, and grumbling. This will cause you to never reach your goal or have a negative outcome.

Learning how to drive the bus is the next strategy that I want to share with you. Of course, I do not mean that you need to learn how to drive a real bus, but instead, you need to know how to get the people on board who are in alignment with your vision and then you need to know how to use their skills and talents to ensure they are in the proper position to contribute to the fulfillment of the vision. There will be times when you are given a group of people and you do not have to worry about getting anyone on board because what you are doing is some type of assigned task, but more often than not, you are going to have to recruit people to work within your group.

Either way, you are going to have to understand how to get them to accept the vision you have and to feel a personal connection to that vision. You are the bus driver and you have to get the passengers onto the bus before you can ever leave the station. Once you have the passengers or your group together, it is time to understand what skills and talents each of them have.

This is one of the most important things you can do because you do not want someone's skills or talents going to waste when they could be what makes your project a success. You will need to take a bit of time to assess the skills and talents of everyone in the group. Once you have that information, you will be able to assign tasks to each person in the group based on what will allow them to use the skills and talents they possess.

Imagine that you are leading a line in a factory and you have four people on your line. One of them is very fast at boxing the product, one of them has a great eye for detail, another has the ability to load the line quickly, and the fourth one is great at getting labels on the product. You find all of this out when you are assessing their skills and talents. If you had not spent the time it takes to assess the skills and talents of the group you are leading, you may end up with the quality guy loading the line, the loading guy placing labels on the product, the label guy boxing the product, and the packer working in quality.

Not assessing the skills and talents of those who are in your group will not only cause them to be placed in the wrong position, where they are unable to use the skills and talents they have to the best of their ability, but, in this case, it would also slow production and it could cause poor quality product. In the end, it could cause the entire vision to be lost and for the group to fail completely. This is why it is important for you to understand your role as a leader. One very small, simple decision you fail to make could cause the complete failure of the entire group.

Filling the void is the next strategy and if you have not noticed yet, it is important for you to use *all* of these strategies, not just one. As the leader, if you want to be as successful leader, it is up to you to communicate with your group on an ongoing basis. You need to be there to answer questions, to help keep the attitude positive, and to push everyone closer to the vision you have. Now is not the time to sit at your desk, read emails, or return phone calls. You need to be with your group to lead them. When one of the members of your group begins to fall, you need to be there to pick them up and keep the group together and focused. That is your job, not dictating every move each person should make.

Finally, you need to make sure that you can talk about the important issues and that you do so often. A true leader is not afraid of having difficult discussions with difficult people, they are not afraid of telling the members of their group when something is not working, and they are not afraid of their voice to be heard. When I say this, I want to remind you that this does not mean you need to raise your voice or get an attitude with the members of your group. It simply means that you need to be mature enough to talk to those who are in your group about the things that matter. You also need to make sure you are able to handle any situation that would arise such as members not getting along or not wanting to work together. This is when you will need to take control and be able to bring the group back together and focus them on the task at hand.

To finish up this chapter, I want to talk about a few more techniques you can use to ensure that you are a successful leader. The first thing I want to talk about is ensuring that you provide clear expectations for your group as well as for each member of the group. If you want to be a truly successful leader, then you need to make sure everyone in your group knows what is expected of them. This is when you can go into extreme detail and not have to worry about becoming a dictator instead of a leader. There is nothing sadder than a group of people who know they can reach a specific goal, but none of them have been given any direction and do not know what they are responsible for. Make sure you break everything down and be willing to answer any questions the members may have.

Second, you want to make sure that the members of your group have the tools they need to succeed. If a new piece of technology is acquired, you need to make sure the members are shown how to use the technology and that they are shown how to use it in a way that will ensure their success. One example of this might be that several new programs have been purchased for a group of people who are in charge of tracking the finances of a company. The members go to a course to learn how to use the new programs, but instead of being taught how to use Excel, for example, they are taught how to use Word. This is an example of improper training and it will lead to the failure of the group as a whole and the failure of each individual.

Next, you need to ensure that you are recognizing when a job has been well done. I have mentioned giving compliments for accomplishments a few times, but it cannot be said enough. When you have a specific member of the group who is going above and beyond what has been asked of them, make sure you acknowledge this. You should also make sure that you acknowledge when the entire group is doing a good job. More than just an acknowledgement, you will want to thank the group and maybe even give them some type of reward.

If the group you are leading is a group of employees and not a group of people who have signed up to be part of the group, you will need to get them interested in what the overall goal is. This can be difficult at times because many people want to make their money and go home at the end of the day. They do not want to become involved in any other activity at work, but if you learn how to sell your idea and show the employees that they will get some type of pay off in the end, chances are, they are going to work hard on your project. Even if the payoff is simply being able to place something new on their resume or even a free meal once the goal is accomplished, people will tend to work harder and get on board a lot quicker if you can get them interested in some way. Of course, you do not want people in your group who are only interested in getting a free meal so you need to show them that they will be making a difference and that they will be recognized as well.

Always make sure that you value the opinions of those who are in the group. You are in charge of leading the group but if you wanted everything done your way, then you would not have a group at all, you would simply do it all yourself. You need to make sure that you are open to hearing what the members have to say and taking it all into consideration. I have seen companies save millions of dollars because they listened to the opinions of the employees. Remember, these are the people who are out there doing what needs to be done each day. They see how things work and they usually know more about how things work than those who are in their offices. Listening to their opinions will not only make them feel respected, but it could also actually benefit you in the long run.

Help the members of your group move forward. Ensure that they are able to take courses, if they are interested, that will help not only them in the future, but also help meet the goals of the entire group or company. Don't feel as if you need to hold people back to keep them around. Instead, help them grow and you will find that once this happens, these people become more loyal to your vision, your group, or your company.

Always make sure that you are communicating the progress that is being made. Often times, when a group of people is working toward a specific goal, they are not informed of the progress that is being made and this makes them lose sight of the goal. Instead, make sure the members know exactly what is going on. Set daily goals for them to reach and you will find that as you communicate the progress toward these goals, those who are in the group will work even harder to reach the goal simply because they know what they need to do and they know that their progress is important.

Make partners out of those who are in your group. This is especially good for employees. People want to make a difference and they want to feel like they are part of something bigger than themselves. They want responsibility and they want to feel proud of what they have done. When you make partners out of those who are in your group, you are telling them that not only are they equal to you, but they are also part of the bigger picture, that without them, the entire project would fail.

Think about Wal-Mart, for example. This company partners with its employees, they tell the employees that they are part owner of the company. The majority of the employees at Wal-Mart take that into themselves and behave as if they are part owners. They want to make sure that no one is ripping them off, other employees are doing their jobs, and that, in the end, Wal-Mart is making a profit so that they are making a profit. Now you do not have to go as far as Wal-Mart does with this, simply telling people that they are the owner of whatever area they are responsible for is enough for them to take on that same responsibility.

Those are the steps to becoming a great leader, the strategies that successful leaders use, and the techniques you can use to help you become a successful leader.

When it really comes down to it, yes, being a leader can be difficult, but if you are a good leader, one who follows the tips that you have learned in this chapter, you will find that those you are leading are actually doing the majority of the work and that is what being a leader is supposed to look like.

Chapter 4 - Tips for Being a Great Leader

I could write thousands of pages that talk about how a person could be a great leader, but that would simply be too much information for one person to deal with, so in this chapter, I want to give you some short tips that will help you to become the leader you were born to be.

1. Always be confident, but not arrogant. Many people confuse the two, but for you to be confident when you are leading, you need to ensure that you know what you are talking about. You also need to ensure that when you speak, you do so with confidence.

2. Never rely on the knowledge or judgement of others. Instead, you need to make sure you know what you are talking about and although it is important to listen to other peoples' opinions, you need to make sure you do your own research before you decide that they are correct.

3. Being a successful leader is all about having a vision. If you do not have a vision, then those you are leading will not have a vision and there is no way that you will ever be able to reach your goals.

4. If you want to be a great leader, then you need to learn how to inspire others. I always suggest that leaders take a few psychology courses so they can understand how the human mind works. This will help you to inspire those who are in your group, but if you cannot take the time to take these courses, simply inspiring them with your own work will do. Get out there and become the inspiration your group needs.

5. If you are going to be a leader, you need to be ambitious and you need to be able to take risks. A great leader does not hide in the corner and fear risk-taking, instead, they are out there doing what needs to be done and testing their limits.

6. Never allow anyone to tell you that you cannot do something. I have often said that if you tell me I can't do something, I will go out and do it just to prove you wrong. This is the mindset we all need to have. You are the only person who decides what you can and cannot do and by allowing others to set limits for you, you are allowing them to lead you, instead of you leading them.

7. A true leader is an organized person. There is no way you can lead a group of people if you are not organized. You have to know where all of your notes are, you have to be

able to find the information that is needed when it is needed, and you need to be able to lead by example. If you are not organized, there is no way your group is going to be organized and without organization, the project will fail.

8. You have to learn how to handle stress. I remember working for a company and the boss would turn red when he became stressed, and he would run his hand through his hair so much, it would stand on end. This became a joke to the employees and they began doing whatever they could to get him stressed whenever they could. There was no respect for him because he was not able to handle the stress caused by small issue and everyone knew he could not handle the stress if a large issue had occurred. That is not how a successful leader behaves. If you struggle with handling stress, I suggest you work on that before anything else. You can talk to a counselor or you can learn through books, but you need to focus on your coping skills before you try to lead a group of people.

9. I already told you that communication is key, but what I did not tell you is that there is more to it than just listening to what the members of your group have to say. You have to be able to articulate what you are

thinking as well as what you would like to see done. If you are an introvert, chances are, you are going to struggle with this. You have to be able to speak to a group of people without losing your nerve.

10.   Committing to your own plan is vital if you want to be a strong leader. Many times, people will come up with a plan, think that it is a good idea, and then pass it off for the group to handle while not being involved. You have to commit to your plan if you want to get anyone else to commit to it. You have to show that your idea is important to you if you want others to make it important to them. If you lack commitment, then it is guaranteed that those you are leading are going to lack commitment as well.

11. Whatever you are working on has to solve a problem. If you create a vision that does not address a problem, then there is not a goal to work toward. You need to be able to discuss the problem with your group and focus on solving that specific problem. Other issues may arise along the way and you can make note of them, but you need to make sure your focus stays on dealing with the specific problem your vision addresses.

12. Be able to acknowledge your own weaknesses. Knowing what your weaknesses

are will allow you to find members in your group to help fill in the gaps. Remember in the beginning of this book when I told you that you do not have to have all of the qualities that I would talk about if you wanted to be a successful leader? This is why you do not have to have them. If you struggle with organization, then find a member of your team who excels at it. If you are unable to admit that you do have your own weaknesses, your group will not be successful.

13. A true leader is fair. We are all human and we have people who we tend to want to trust more than others. We have favorites and we would rather listen to our friends than anyone else but when you are a leader, you have to forget all of that and learn how to be fair to everyone. You have to understand that everyone in your group matters and even if you do not like the person at all, you have to be willing to listen to what they have to say.

14. Be resourceful. When you are a leader, you are not always going to have all of the answers and there are going to be times when you try something and it simply does not work out. When this happens, you need to be willing to try another method. You cannot allow the feeling of failure to stop

you and you cannot be afraid of failure. You need to remember that not everything is going to work out every time and remind yourself that you don't know everything there is to know. If you can't come up with an idea on your own, be willing to discuss it with the entire group.

15. Be positive. I remember learning about The Secret a few years ago and I thought it was a bunch of silliness until I realized that what I expected to happen was generally what happened. If I expected failure, that was what I received and if I expected to be successful, I was successful.

16. Don't be serious all of the time. Be silly, be energetic, and be happy. You are the leader, but this does not mean that you have to be a downer all of the time. People tend to relate better with leaders who allow them to see who they really are at least some of the time. Don't be afraid to laugh with your group and don't be afraid to show them your real personality.

17. Understand that there are going to be times when people will not be able to meet their obligations and that is okay, but you also need to be willing to talk to them to find out why they have not done what they were supposed to. When people join your group,

they are saying that they will do what they need to do to help you reach your goals, and when they do not fulfill the responsibilities you have given them it can be frustrating but you need to understand when action is needed and when it is not. One example of when it is not is if someone's child was ill or if they were ill. When action is needed is when the person is simply not doing what they said they would do with no legitimate reason as to why they couldn't.

18.   A great leader will always have someone they can turn to for help. This is known as the leader's right hand man or woman. This person is in charge of catching anything that you miss and helps to carry the load when things become challenging.

19. Never assume. This was something that a teacher taught me while I was in high school and it is something that has stuck with me throughout the years. You should never assume that those who are in your group are working on the project or that they are doing the things that need to be done. Never assume that things are going as planned. Always make sure you have the data to back up everything.

20.   Believe in the people who are in your group and make sure that they know that

you believe in them. Knowing that your leader believes in you and is not going behind your back, making sure that you are doing what you are supposed to be doing, is very important when you are working on a team. You need to know that your leader believes you will do a good job and this will cause the people in your group to push their limits to do what you need them to do.

Of course, we could go on and on, page after page, with tips that you can use to be a successful leader but I feel that these are the most important things for you to do. If you follow all of these tips as well as all of the other information you have been given in this book, you are going to be the leader you were born to be and you are going to be successful when it comes to leading.

Chapter 5 - Always Improving

You may be sitting there and thinking to yourself that this is simply too much for you to do, that there are too many changes that need to be made, and that you will never be the leader you dream of being but that couldn't be farther from the truth.

Simply having the desire to be a strong leader is the first step when it comes to being a successful leader but you need to ask yourself why you want to be a good leader. Do you want to be a good leader because it will get you recognition? Maybe you are looking for some type of power and feel that this is the way for you to get it or maybe you just want a pay raise.

Those are all terrible reasons for you to want to become a leader. If, on the other hand, you want to become a leader because you want to help people make a difference, if you want to lead your company or group into a new direction, or if you want to see others succeed, then you understand what it really is to be a leader.

Earlier in this book, I talked about serving as a leader and that is how you really need to look at it. Being a leader is a way you can help to serve those in your company or group as well as the group or company as a whole.

When you look at Webster's dictionary, it states that a leader is someone with the ability to lead, but I believe that being a leader is much more than that. To be a great leader, you must be able to inspire as well as control a group of people, ensuring that they maintain focus on the task at hand.

This is important because if you want to be a leader, then you need to think like a leader. If you do not truly understand what a leader is, then there is no possible way for you to think like one. So instead of thinking like someone who has the ability to lead others, you will want to think like someone who has the ability to inspire, control, and ensure that a group of people maintains focus.

President Reagan once said that once a leader has been convinced that a course of action is the correct one, they must be determined to stick to it and never waver when things get tough. This is the mindset you need to have if you want to be a successful leader.

Once you have this mindset, you will be able to go through this book and pick out areas that you know you need to work on. Remember when we talked about understanding your own weaknesses? This is when you need to be honest with yourself and determine where your weaknesses are as a leader. Choose a few areas to work on and follow the tips I have given you.

Once you begin seeing improvement in those areas, you will be able to move on and work on new areas of improvement. This should never stop. You should never think that you are such a great leader that you no longer to improve upon yourself and that you are as good as you can get.

It is that type of thinking that is done by some of the worst leaders I have ever met. When you have worked through all of the tips in this book, and this should take you a very long time, then you can grab a more advanced book and begin working through it or you can simply start over and begin improving upon the skills you learned in this book.

The point is, this is a never ending process, and as long as you are a leader, you should continue to work on your leadership skills. You should always work to improve your leadership ability and only then will you find that you are the leader you were meant to be.

While you are working on your leadership skills, consider looking at other areas of your life that need improvement and work on them as well. There are many areas in all of our lives that can benefit from what we learn when we are trying to become good leaders and you should take the skills you have learned and apply them to other areas of your life as well.

Doing this will not only help you to build your leadership skills, but it will help to reduce the stress in your life and help you to have the life you want. Practicing your leadership skills at home will help you when you use them at work, but it will also help to ensure that you live in a peaceful home and that you are able to do the things you want to do.

As you focus on different areas of leadership, incorporate the same principles into your entire life because after all, we don't stop being leaders just because we leave the office.

Conclusion

Becoming a great leader can be a very satisfying accomplishment if done correctly. I hope this book was able to shed some light on the different ways of thinking that lead to successful leadership as well as provide a good resource of techniques and strategies to lead effectively. It's not always going to be easy to be an easy task, however you can greatly improve you leading skills by taking what you've learned and applying it towards your own life. The possibilities are endless as long as you stay determined and never give up!

I hope that this book was able to help you attain leadership attitude you were born with and forever change your life.

Thank you again for buying this book!

Steve Williams

Related Reading

I have the perfect complement to this book on leadership to further help you with your career goals. Many of you that bought this book to help portray leadership skills are also in search of a job. Being able to display yourself as a great leader is definitely a step in the right direction, however you must have the job interview first before you can do that. Taking the time to perfect your resume can make all the difference in how many interviews you get and subsequently how many job offers you receive.

I highly recommend you check out my book, '*The Winning Resume – Get Hired Today With These Groundbreaking Resume Secrets*'. It is available on Amazon in paperback and digital format.

Scan The Above Code or Go Here to View on Amazon:

http://www.amazon.com/dp/B014LM7M9Y

Stop... Before you close this book, get your free bonus...

Scan Above to Claim Bonus

Or Go To: http://bit.ly/1NKyFuQ

101 Life Success Tips – Start Accomplishing Your Goals Today!
Steve Williams is a motivational expert who has helped thousands of people accomplish their dreams and goals. Here are a few tips he has learned along the way to improving success in his life quickly.

----

1. **Use Visualization.** Visualize what your life will be like when you accomplish your goals. If you cannot see yourself accomplishing your goals, then chances are, you will not accomplish them. Remember

that you are to keep your eye on the prize at the end of the road. There will be times when you feel as if you are stuck and that you are not making any progress toward your goal, but what you need to do when this happens is to remember what your life will be like in 6 months or a year if you continue to work toward your goals. Spend a few minutes with your eyes closed, visualizing how great you will feel and all of the changes that will take place in your life once you reach these goals.

2. **Read Books, a Lot of Books.** For each of these tips, there is a book out there that will give you deeper insight into each tip. Spend time reading each and every day. This will not only exercise your brain and help you learn, but it will also help to relieve the stress you have to deal with on a daily basis. Even if you are not reading a book about self-improvement, make sure you take some time each day to read. Reading fiction books helps to release the creativity we have within ourselves, which can help you solve problems down the road.

3. **Accept That You are Responsible for Your Life.** You are in charge of your life, no one else. You cannot blame your failures on your parents or on what happened to you when you were in high school. You need to

work through any issues you may have but while doing so, understand that no one makes your life what it is except you. If you are not succeeding in life, no one has caused this except for you and when you are successful, you will have no one to thank for it but yourself.

4. **Learn How to Accept Failure and** *Learn* **from It**. Failure, it is something that all of us will face at one point in our lives, no matter what we do to avoid it. You have two choices when it comes to failure. You can either allow the failure to upset you and stop you in your tracks, or you can learn from the failure and change what you do in the future. One example of this may be that you are trying to lose weight, you are tempted by a chocolate cake, and end up eating all of it. Now you have failed. You can either choose to give up on your weight loss goals and eat lots of chocolate cake in the following days, which will most likely cause you to gain more weight, or you can learn from your mistake, understand that you lack the will power to stop eating after a small piece of chocolate cake, avoid it in the future, and move on with your diet and weight loss plan.

5. **Do the Things You Dread the Most First.** No matter what it is that you want to do, you should always do the things that you

dread the most first. This is called eating the frog. This way you are not putting these tasks off while finishing up more enjoyable tasks, you simply do them, get them out of the way, and then you can move on to the tasks you will enjoy more.

This is a brand new report that will show you 101 quick ways to improve your life success. These are just a sample. You can have the entire report for free.

Check Out My Other Books

Below, you'll find some of my other popular books on Amazon and Kindle. Simply scan the link below to visit my author page on Amazon to see my works.

Direct Link - http://www.amazon.com/Steve-Williams/e/B0125EAWUQ/

The Winning Resume – Get Hired Today With These Groundbreaking Resume Secrets

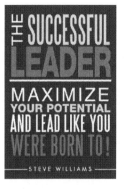

The Successful Leader – Maximize Your Potential And Lead Like You Were Born To!

The Successful Interview – 7 Secrets You Didn't Know About Landing Your Dream Job

The Winners Attitude – Learn How Winners Think to Achieve Success in Life

Quit Smoking Today! The Most Painless Ways to Permanently Stop Smoking

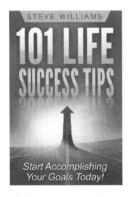

101 Life Success Tips – Start Accomplishing Your Goals Today!

If the links do not work, for whatever reason, you can simply search for these titles on the Amazon website to find them.

64956263R00034

Made in the USA
Lexington, KY
25 June 2017